D1268663

L. E. SMOOT MEMORIAL LIBRARY
9533 KINGS HIGHWAY
KING GEORGE, VA. 22485

B
O
S
T
O
N

RICHARD RAMBECK

THE HISTORY OF THE
RED SOX

CREATIVE EDUCATION

Published by Creative Education
123 South Broad Street, Mankato, Minnesota 56001
Creative Education is an imprint of The Creative Company

Designed by Rita Marshall
Editorial assistance by Tracey Cramer & John Nichols

Photos by: Allsport, Photography, AP/Wide World, Corbis-Bettmann,
Fotosport, SportsChrome.

Copyright © 1999 Creative Education.
International copyrights reserved in all countries.
No part of this book may be reproduced in any form without written
permission from the publisher.
Printed in the United States of America.

Library of Congress Cataloging-in-Publication Data

Rambeck, Richard.
The History of the Boston Red Sox / by Richard Rambeck.
p. cm. — (Baseball)
Summary: Highlights the key personalities and memorable games in the
history of the team that began playing in 1901 under the name Boston
Pilgrims.
ISBN: 0-88682-900-3

1. Boston Red Sox (Baseball team)—History—Juvenile literature.
[1. Boston Red Sox (Baseball team)—History. 2. Baseball—History.]
I. Title. II. Series: Baseball (Mankato, Minn.)

GV875.B62R355 1999
796.357'64'0974461—dc21   97-6344

First edition

9 8 7 6 5 4 3 2 1

The city of Boston is known as the "Hub"—short for the "Hub of the Universe"—because it boasts some of this country's best schools, libraries, and museums. Boston, the capital of Massachusetts, was also a hub of activity during the Revolutionary War.

The activity began in 1770 when British soldiers fired into a Boston mob and killed five people. In 1773, a group of colonists was so upset at what it considered unfair taxation by the British that it threw crates of tea off a British ship into Boston Harbor. The incident became known as the Boston Tea Party. Two years later, Paul Revere made his legendary

Pitcher Cy Young—in an unfamiliar pose.

Behind the pitching of Cy Young, the Pilgrims won their first game ever, defeating Philadelphia 12–4.

midnight ride through the Boston area to warn citizens that British soldiers were coming to destroy the colonists' guns and ammunition supply.

Clearly, Boston is a city rich in history and tradition, and part of that tradition is a professional baseball team known as the Boston Red Sox, a club that began playing in 1901.

As was common at that time, the club was known by several different names. During its first six seasons, Bostonians referred to their team as the "Americans," "Somersets," "Speed Boys," "Plymouth Rocks," and "Puritans," but the most popular name of the time was the "Pilgrims." Boston was one of the charter members of the American League, and the Pilgrims were an immediate success. The club finished second in the American League in 1901, third in 1902, and won the championship in 1903. Boston then defeated the National League winners, the Pittsburgh Pirates, five games to three to become the first champions of professional baseball. In 1907, the team name was changed to the Red Sox because the players' uniforms featured bright red socks—a bold fashion statement in a time when most teams wore gray flannel uniforms.

The early Boston teams were built around great pitchers, the most famous of whom was Denton "Cy" Young. He joined Boston in 1901 when he was 34 years old and pitched eight years for the team. During his remarkable career, which spanned 21 seasons with five teams, Young won 511 games, easily the most ever by a pitcher and a record that may stand forever (no other pitcher has even won 400 games). He had an amazing 14 straight seasons with 20 or more victories. Young once commented to a young sportswriter, "Sonny, I've

Hard-hitting outfielder Troy O'Leary.

1 9 1 2

Fenway Park opened, named for its location in the Fenway section of Boston.

won more major-league games than you've ever seen." Young retired before World War I, but his legend lives on to this day. The annual trophy for being the best pitcher in each league bears his name—the Cy Young Award.

Cy Young was the best-known Boston pitcher in the early years, but he wasn't the team's only great hurler. "Big" Bill Dinneen, "Long" Tom Hughes, and Jesse Tannehill each won more than 20 games at least once. Then in 1908, a new pitching star joined the Red Sox. His name was "Smokey Joe" Wood. He won 23 games in 1911 and then posted an incredible 34–5 record in 1912, leading the Red Sox to the American League pennant.

The Red Sox won the AL championship in their first season in Fenway Park, which replaced the team's Huntington Avenue Grounds in 1912. Fenway Park remains the home field of the Red Sox to this day. The team celebrated its first season in Fenway in grand style, beating the National League champion New York Giants four games to three in the World Series. The Red Sox didn't stop there. They won World Series titles in 1915, 1916, and 1918. Again, pitching was the key, and the team had a new star: George Herman Ruth, better known as "Babe." Ruth pitched 16 scoreless innings in the 1916 series and 13 more scoreless innings in the 1918 series.

After the 1918 World Series, Ruth asked Boston owner Harry Frazee to switch him to the outfield so he could concentrate on hitting. Frazee initially refused Ruth's request, but outfielder Harry Hooper talked Frazee into giving Ruth a chance. Ruth moved to the outfield, but sadly, most of the Boston stars, including Ruth, soon moved to other teams.

Frazee, who bought the Red Sox in 1917, made a habit of selling his star players to the New York Yankees to support his financially troubled Frazee Theatre in New York, located near the Yankees' office. The list of Red Sox stars Frazee sold to the Yankees is a long one, and it is topped by Babe Ruth. A popular myth in Boston states that after Ruth was sold to the Yankees, he put a hex on the Red Sox to ensure they would never win a World Series without him. The "Curse of the Bambino" as Boston fans called it, has dogged the team ever since. Thanks partly to Frazee, the Yankees built a dynasty, becoming the dominant team in the American League. The Red Sox, however, fell into a slump that lasted nearly 20 years. In fact, from 1919 to 1937, Boston never finished higher than fourth in the American League. In nine of those years, the once-mighty Red Sox finished last.

Jimmie Foxx launched a Boston club-record 50 home runs during the season.

WILLIAMS IS AN IMMEDIATE HIT

Things started to improve for the Red Sox after Thomas A. Yawkey bought the team in 1933. Yawkey's ownership style was the opposite of Frazee's. Frazee sold players; Yawkey bought them. Yawkey's first major acquisition was a pair of brothers, catcher Rick Ferrell and pitcher Wes Ferrell. Yawkey then bartered with the Philadelphia Athletics and came away with two future Hall-of-Famers: pitcher Lefty Grove and slugger Jimmie Foxx. Yawkey then shocked other American League owners by spending $250,000 to bring Washington Senators star Joe Cronin to the Boston organization. Cronin came as a player but later became manager of the Boston Red Sox.

Another Boston great, Dwight Evans.

Five-time AL batting champ, Wade Boggs. 11

Ted Williams was named the AL Most Valuable Player as he led the Red Sox to the pennant.

While Yawkey was buying players, the Red Sox were also developing such home-grown stars as Bobby Doerr, Johnny Pesky, Dom DiMaggio, and a skinny outfielder named Ted Williams, who joined the Red Sox in 1939. Red Sox veterans looked at the 6-foot-3 and 150-pound Williams and shook their heads. They almost laughed out loud when they saw him run the bases; Williams, with his bouncing gallop, looked as if he was skipping rope.

Williams was awkward, but he was also very confident. "All I want out of life," he said when he made the major leagues, "is that when I walk down the street, folks will say, 'There goes the greatest hitter who ever lived.'" The other Red Sox noticed his confidence and kidded the rookie at every opportunity. "Wait'll you see Foxx hit, kid," one of them said to Williams, to which he replied, "Wait until Foxx sees me hit."

It didn't take Williams long to become a star and one of the best hitters in the American League. In 1941, only his third season in the big leagues, he hit an amazing .400 for most of the year. Coming into the last day of the regular season, his batting average was exactly .400. By not playing in the season-ending doubleheader, Williams could easily have preserved his .400 average, but the man they called "the Kid" would have none of that. "I don't want anyone ever saying that I made my .400 batting average by hiding in the dugout," Williams said. He played both games of the doubleheader, going six-for-eight to finish with a .406 average. It remains the last time a major-league player has hit .400 or better in a season.

Despite the heroics of Williams and other stars, the Red

Sox didn't win a pennant until the 1946 season. That was the year the Red Sox were reunited after several of them, including Williams, served their country during World War II. The Red Sox blended good hitting—always a team trademark—with solid pitching, which was led by Dave "Boo" Ferriss, to win 104 games and claim the American League title. In the World Series, though, the Red Sox lost to the St. Louis Cardinals four games to three. The Boston fans had waited 28 years to cheer for an American League champion. Unfortunately, after 1946, they would wait 21 more years for the next pennant winner.

Lefthanded ace Mel Parnell blanked the White Sox, 4–0, on his way to a no-hitter.

After the success of 1946, the Red Sox slumped to third in the American League in 1947, followed by two second-place finishes in 1948 and 1949. Red Sox fans started to get frustrated, and they took out much of their frustration on Williams, even though he led the American League in homers in 1947 and 1949 and won the batting championship in 1947 and 1948. In addition, Williams won the Triple Crown honor in 1947 by leading the league in homers, batting average, and runs batted in. (He also won the Triple Crown in 1942.)

Despite Williams's outstanding play, he was booed in Boston almost as much as he was cheered. The fans had high expectations for the team, and they were disappointed when the Red Sox and Williams couldn't win pennants. Between 1950 and 1966, the Red Sox never finished higher than third in the American League. Williams, though, continued to star for the team throughout the 1950s. In all, Williams won six American League batting titles, the last in 1958. Two years later he retired, but not before hitting a memorable home run in Fenway Park in his last at-bat.

1 9 6 8

Ken "Hawk" Harrelson led the Red Sox with 35 homers and a league-leading 109 RBIs.

When Williams bid farewell to the Boston fans after hitting his homer, they gave him a long standing ovation. Even though many of them had booed Williams during his career, all of them knew how special he was. His 521 career homers and 2,654 hits are all the more impressive knowing Williams lost nearly five seasons of his career to military service both in World War II and Korea. Many fans wondered if Boston would ever have another player like him again. Then, just a year later, in 1961, Boston had a new left fielder, a player some were calling the next Ted Williams. That player was Carl Yastrzemski.

YAZ JAZZES UP THE SOX

Yastrzemski, who was known as "Yaz," wasn't a clone of Ted Williams. Yaz wasn't as tall, and he didn't have Williams's strength or power, but he did have a smooth left-handed swing. Like Williams, Yaz won an American League batting title in only his third year in major league baseball (1963). Yaz was one of the top hitters in the American League almost every year; however, the Red Sox still weren't one of the top teams. Actually, they were among the worst—at least until 1967.

Despite the presence of Yastrzemski and several new young stars—Boston native outfielder Tony Conigliaro, first baseman George Scott, and pitcher Jim Lonborg—the Red Sox slumped to ninth in the 10-team American League in 1966. A year later, though, everything fell into place for the Red Sox and young manager Dick Williams. Conigliaro and Scott hit for power, although Conigliaro's season would be

Catcher Carlton Fisk.

"Yaz"—Carl Yastrzemski.

cut short in August after he was hit in the eye by a wild pitch from the Angels' Jack Hamilton. And Lonborg became the first Boston hurler to win the prestigious American League Cy Young Award.

But nobody had a better year than Yaz. His .326 average, 44 homers, and 121 RBIs were good enough to make him the first American Leaguer in 11 years to win the Triple Crown.

1 9 7 2

Luis Aparicio joined Carl Yastrzemski, Carlton Fisk, and Reggie Smith on the AL All-Star team.

"I remember saying to my wife," Yastrzemski said, "that if we had sat down every day and planned situations in which I could be the hero, at bat and on the field, we couldn't have come closer than what actually happened." Yaz was the hero all season for the Red Sox, who won the American League pennant on the final day of the regular season with a victory over Minnesota.

For the first time since 1946, the Red Sox were in the World Series. As in 1946, their opponent was St. Louis, and also as in 1946, Boston lost four games to three, dropping the seventh game of the series in front of the screaming fans at Fenway Park. Despite their disappointment, the fans cheered loudly for the Red Sox after the game ended. They were cheering for a remarkable team that had gone from second-to-last to American League champs in one year.

Although the Red Sox wouldn't duplicate their status as league champions until 1975, Yastrzemski was still a star, winning the 1968 American League batting crown. Sadly, Tony Conigliaro, who actually was leading the American League in home runs in 1967 before his terrible injury, never regained the form that made him one of the brightest young stars in baseball. Additionally, Jim Lonborg never had another year to compare with his Cy Young season of 1967.

1 9 8 3

After 23 seasons with the Red Sox, Carl Yastrzemski retired with a career batting average of .285.

The Red Sox, however, built a stable of new stars. Catcher Carlton Fisk won the Rookie of the Year award in the American League in 1972. Three years later, the Red Sox added two more rookies—Fred Lynn and Jim Rice—who turned the club from a merely good one into a pennant contender. During the 1975 season, Rice hit .309 with 22 home runs and 102 RBIs. Center fielder Lynn had an even better year; he batted .331 and was named both Rookie of the Year and Most Valuable Player in the American League.

Led by Lynn, Rice, Fisk, and pitcher Luis Tiant, the Red Sox won the East Division of the American League in 1975. (The AL was divided into two divisions in 1969—the East and the West.) Boston then defeated AL West champion Oakland three games to none to claim the American League pennant and advance to the World Series. The Red Sox had to play in the series without Rice, who broke his wrist late in the season. Despite this handicap, Boston still gave National League champion Cincinnati fits. Five of the seven games in the series were decided by one run, including both the sixth and seventh games.

The Red Sox trailed in the series three games to two before the sixth game, which was played in Boston. In that game, Boston overcame a Cincinnati lead and eventually won by a score of 7–6 on a dramatic homer by Fisk in the 12th inning. In the seventh game, Cincinnati broke a 3–3 tie with a run in the top of the ninth and went on to win the game and the series.

Three years later, the Red Sox battled the New York Yankees down to the last day of the regular season for the AL East crown. The two teams wound up tied for first and had to meet in a one-game playoff at Fenway Park. Boston fans were shocked when light-hitting New York shortstop Bucky Dent popped a fly ball over the storied 37-foot high "Green Monster" wall in left field for a home run that buried the Red Sox and sent the Yankees into the American League Championship Series.

It was to be the last chance for Carl Yastrzemski to play on a pennant-winning team. Yaz, who retired after the 1983 season, became the only American Leaguer ever to hit at least 400 home runs and accumulate at least 3,000 base hits. Babe Ruth, Mickey Mantle, Joe DiMaggio, Ty Cobb, and Ted Williams were each unable to do what Yastrzemski did. "He's a true superstar," said the Yankees' Reggie Jackson. "You really have to have other athletes comment on what he has achieved, because you can't really appreciate what it means to perform as he has for as long as he has."

Frank Robinson, another superstar, was equally impressed by Yastrzemski. "It's a great accomplishment to blend power with consistency," said Robinson, who is fourth on the all-time home-run list with 586. "When I was playing in the league, he was the only one I considered a true superstar." When Yastrzemski retired, the Red Sox already had a new young hitter with superstar potential ready to follow in the footsteps of Yaz and Williams. The newcomer's name was Wade Boggs.

For the second time in three years, Wade Boggs led the AL in hitting, batting an incredible .368.

BOGGS AND THE "ROCKET" SPARK SOX TO SUCCESS

When Boggs, a third baseman, joined the team in the early 1980s, the Red Sox already had a player in that

"The Rocket Man"—Roger Clemens.

position, Carney Lansford, who was an excellent hitter and had won the 1981 American League batting title. But everybody knew Boggs was also a great hitter, so the Red Sox decided to trade Lansford and give Boggs a shot at starting. He didn't disappoint. In 1983, his first full year as a starter, Boggs won the American League batting title. In fact, Boggs won five batting titles in the six years between 1983 and 1988.

What made Boggs such a good hitter? Two things stand out: his concentration and his preparation. When batting, Boggs concentrated so hard on the pitcher, he went into a trance-like state he called a "cocoon." "When I'm in the cocoon," Boggs said, "I can eliminate distractions and variables and shut out the entire world except for me and the pitcher. I don't like surprises. I face enough of the unexpected when I'm hitting. I don't need any others."

Boggs was also superstitious. His pregame meal always consisted of chicken. "Red meat dulls the reflexes," explained the eight-time All-Star. Along with Boggs, Boston also featured one of the most-feared pitchers in the game: "Rocket" Roger Clemens. The big, Texas-born right-hander joined the Red Sox in 1984 and immediately impressed his teammate Boggs. "When I first saw Roger, it was spring training, and I saw him warm up and thought, 'Thank God that guy is on our team,'" laughed the third baseman. Clemens possessed the wicked combination of blazing fastball and nasty demeanor that chilled the hearts of opposing hitters.

"He throws so hard that even when you know the heat's coming, you can't hit it," grumbled the Royals' Steve Balboni. Clemens's heat was so dominating that he struck

1 9 9 1

Led by center fielder Ellis Burks, the Red Sox were one of the AL's best teams.

Talented All-Star Mike Greenwell.

out 20 batters in a game on two occasions, 10 years apart (1986 against Seattle and 1996 against Detroit).

In 1986, the Red Sox, led by Clemens and Boggs, stormed to the AL East division crown with a record of 95–66. After battling past the California Angels in a tense, seven-game American League Championship series, the Red Sox would face the mighty New York Mets in the World Series. After taking a three-games-to-two series lead, the Red Sox looked ready to bring home the championship with Clemens pitching game six. But after seven innings, a weary Clemens left the game leading 3–2. A Mets rally in the eighth inning tied the game at three, but Boston struck for two scores in the top of the 10th to lead 5–3. Needing only three outs to become world champions, the Red Sox quickly recorded two outs without surrendering a run. But then fate turned cruel for Boston fans.

Amazingly, the Red Sox gave up three runs on three singles, a wild pitch, and an error by first baseman Bill Buckner on a slow-rolling ground ball that allowed the Mets to even the series at three games apiece. Two days later, the heartbroken Red Sox tried gamely but could not recover from their game-six trauma, losing the deciding game seven 8–5. "That's baseball," muttered a stunned Boston manager John McNamara. "This game is my life, but man, it can test you. It can test you. . . . I don't think I'll get over this."

The Red Sox rose to the top of the American League East again in 1988 with an 89–73 mark but were swept four games to none by the Oakland A's in the American League Championship Series. After a third-place season in 1990, the Red Sox used gutsy performances by several key players to

1 9 9 4

Center fielder Otis Nixon stole 42 bases, the most by a Red Sox player since Tommy Harper stole 54 in 1973.

One of baseball's most feared sluggers, Mo Vaughn (pages 26–27).

capture another American League East title in 1990. But once again, the powerful Oakland A's ended Boston's season in the league championship series, this time in a four-game sweep. "I've been on lots of Red Sox teams with more talent than this one," Dwight Evans said during the 1990 season, "but never one with more character." The team's division title run was keyed by the veteran leadership of Clemens, catcher Tony Peña, left fielder Mike Greenwell, and pitcher Mike Boddicker. Such youngsters as Ellis Burks and first baseman Carlos Quintana provided the spark that lifted Boston to the top of the AL East.

1 9 9 5

Powerful infielder John Valentin socked 37 doubles to pace all Red Sox hitters.

"HIT DOG" A BIG HIT IN BOSTON

As the 1990s began, the Red Sox had some of the best talent in baseball. Many fans thought 1991 would be the year the Red Sox would make it to the World Series. The team was bolstered by a bumper crop of talented rookies, including Mo Vaughn, who soon became a key slugger for Boston. However, despite the high expectations and Roger Clemens capturing his third Cy Young Award, Boston finished the season in second place behind Toronto.

Then the team seemed to fall apart. The organization made several ill-advised free-agent signings, conducted some bad trades, and suffered through a rash of injuries to key players. With so many problems to address, Boston finished dead last in its division in 1992 and spent the next couple of years fighting its way back up, finishing fifth in 1993 and fourth in 1994.

By 1995, the Red Sox were hot again. Mo Vaughn had

blossomed into one of the league's most dangerous hitters. His .300 average, 39 home runs, and 129 RBIs were good enough to earn the big first baseman the league's Most Valuable Player award. However, success did not always come easily for Vaughn. He struggled early in his career and was even sent back to the minors in 1992. But in 1993, Vaughn came under the tutelage of Mike Easler, the new Boston hitting coach. Easler, known as the "Hit Man" for his prowess at the plate during his playing career, took the talented but dispirited Vaughn under his wing. "I just wanted Mo to relax up there and have confidence in himself," explained Easler. "Confidence is everything in hitting."

1 9 9 7

AL Rookie of the Year Nomar Garciaparra set an AL rookie record with a 30-game hitting streak.

Before long, Easler's pupil began to apply his lessons well, battering American League pitching. Soon Boston sportswriters noticed the change in Vaughn and nicknamed him the "Hit Dog" in recognition of Easler's influence and Vaughn's new ferocity at the plate. With the Hit Dog belting bombs, Boston again won the AL East crown in 1995, but their World Series dreams were once again snuffed out when the Cleveland Indians defeated them in the league championship series three games to zero.

Although the Red Sox had only mediocre seasons in 1996 and 1997, the team has done a fine job of rebuilding around their superstar Vaughn. Second baseman John Valentin and 1997 AL Rookie of the Year shortstop Nomar Garciaparra formed a brilliant combination both offensively and defensively. "John hit 18 homers for us in 1997, and Nomar hit 30," said a smiling Vaughn. "How many teams got pop like that at second and short? Nobody." As for the pitchers, the Red Sox suffered a loss when Roger Clemens left through

29

L. E. SMOOT MEMORIAL LIBRARY
9533 KINGS HIGHWAY
KING GEORGE, VA 22485

Knuckleball ace Tim Wakefield.

Star second baseman John Valentin.

free agency after the 1996 season, but the team has rebuilt a strong starting rotation with promising youngster Brian Rose, knuckleballer Tim Wakefield, left-hander Butch Henry, and prize free-agent acquisition Pedro Martinez.

1 9 9 8

The Red Sox were looking for big numbers from Troy O'Leary, who got off to a hot start in 1998.

The hard-throwing Martinez captured the 1997 National League Cy Young Award while pitching for the Montreal Expos. His 17–8 record with 305 strikeouts and a 1.90 ERA convinced the Red Sox, who needed a star to replace Clemens, to offer the big money. "Pedro gives us an ace," explained third baseman Tim Naehring. "He's a guy who strikes fear in your heart as a hitter." The Red Sox also hope former star pitcher Bret Saberhagen can revive an injury-plagued career and help the team.

With these solid players in place, Boston fans have high hopes for a World Series championship, something the Red Sox have not claimed since 1918. They've been so close, so many times, losing in seven games in 1946, 1967, 1975, and 1986. Amazingly, such Boston stars as Ted Williams, Jimmie Foxx, Joe Cronin, and Carl Yastrzemski never played on a World Series winner in Boston. Many experts believe it's only a matter of time before the Red Sox end their decades of disappointment and finally bring a World Series title back to Boston.

L.E. SMOOT MEMORIAL LIBRARY

3 1150 1001 8475 9

J
796.357
64
Ram

Rambeck, Richard.
The history of
the Boston Red Sox

WITHDRAWN

Smoot Memorial Library
9533 Kings Highway
King George, VA 22485
540-775-2147   smoot.org

L. E. SMOOT MEMORIAL LIBRARY
KING GEORGE, VA. 22485

GAYLORD R

L. E. SMOOT MEMORIAL LIBRARY
9533 KINGS HIGHWAY
KING GEORGE, VA 22485